ON COMPILING AN
ANNOTATED BIBLIOGRAPHY

ON COMPILING AN ANNOTATED BIBLIOGRAPHY

JAMES L. HARNER

Second Edition

The Modern Language Association of America
New York   2000

For information about obtaining permission to reprint material from
MLA book publications, send your request by mail (see address
below), e-mail (permissions@mla.org), or fax (646-458-0030).

Library of Congress Cataloging-in-Publication Data

Harner, James L.
On compiling an annotated bibliography / James L. Harner.—2nd ed.
p.   cm.
Includes bibliographical references (p.).
ISBN 0-87352-979-0 (pbk.)
1. Bibliography—Methodology. 2. English literature—
Bibliography—Methodology. 3. Abstracting. 4. English literature—
Abstracting and indexing. I. Title.

Z1001.H33   2000
010´.44—dc21   00-038663

Published by The Modern Language Association of America
26 Broadway, New York, NY 10004-1789
www.mla.org

Contents

Preface to the Second Edition

In the nine years since the revised edition of *On Compiling an Annotated Bibliography* was published, the World Wide Web has established itself as the preferred medium for the publication of bibliographies. Like other documents published on the Web, a bibliography can be updated frequently, can be linked to related resources, can be searched by keyword, and is available to anyone with access to a Web browser. But, like so many Web-based data sources, a Web bibliography is usually unrefereed (and not professionally copyedited), frequently incomplete, subject to unannounced alterations, more notable for design than content, and outdated. Since few publishers now are willing even to consider proposals for printed bibliographies and even fewer are interested in including them in fledgling electronic publication programs, it is essential that some kind of vetting process—similar to that exercised by the Modern Language Association's Committee on Scholarly Editions—be established to ensure the quality of electronic bibliographies. Otherwise, one crucial element of the infrastructure of scholarship will continue to deteriorate.

As in the preceding edition, I have availed myself of the opportunity to update and revise some of my recommendations. But, because of the continual evolution of cyberspace, I refrain from discussing specific software. Although the following recommendations were formulated in an era of print bibliographies, they remain essential to the research that must undergird any electronic bibliography.

Because electronic publishing is especially amenable to serial bibliographies, I have received many requests for advice from prospective editors concerning the establishment and maintenance of an ongoing bibliography that is updated at regular intervals. Any reader who wishes advice about serial bibliographies or about annotated bibliographies in general may e-mail me at j-harner@tamu.edu.

Introduction

In recent years, literature scholars and librarians have been inundated with annotated bibliographies, a natural outgrowth of the proliferation of books and articles since the 1960s and, more recently, of the ubiquitous presence of the World Wide Web.[1] Scholars eager for bibliographies that might reduce research time by ordering the mass of scholarship on an author or subject, librarians who felt duty bound to purchase (or subscribe to) nearly any bibliography, and Web surfers, accustomed to locating quickly information in cyberspace, provided a ready audience. Of course, publishers and Web-savvy individuals were not slow to capitalize on this market.

Several of these bibliographies are models of their kind: intelligent, accurate, thorough, efficiently organized works that foster scholarship by guiding readers through accumulated studies as well as implicitly or explicitly isolating dominant scholarly concerns, identifying topics that have been overworked, and suggesting needed research. Unfortunately, many are flawed in either conception or execution, and some are downright shoddy. Numerous shortcomings of annotated bibliographies can be attributed to lax editorial supervision by publishers (some of whom act as little more than vendors who print unedited manuscripts) or the lack of any vetting agency for Web-based bibliographies; however, my experience in compiling, editing, reviewing, and reading annotated bibliographies suggests that most deficiencies result from a compiler's unawareness of basic procedures, potential problems, and research techniques.

Despite the importance of annotated bibliographies, little attention has been given to the theory and practice of preparing such works. Most publishers who frequently issue annotated bibliographies supply authors with a guide that specifies format, illustrates citation style, and defines scope but says nothing about techniques for compiling the work. Web authors typically get no guidance. Isolated comments on aspects of theory and practice appear in bibliographers' apologias[2] or reviews (especially in *Analytical and Enumerative Bibliography, Library, Resources for American Literary Study*, and *Bulletin of Bibliography*),[3] and both Colaianne and Krummel have set forth some of the general principles of annotated bibliography. No one, however, has addressed in detail the practical matters involved in compiling an annotated bibliography.

This state of affairs is hardly surprising. To many, an annotated bibliography is second-class scholarship (or worse, merely inspired clerical drudgery), the kind of work anyone who has passed a graduate-level course in research methods, completed a dissertation, and gained a rudimentary acquaintance with an HTML or XML editor is qualified to do. While most prospective bibliographers—seasoned scholars or neophytes—realize that they must be relentlessly thorough in their search for material, meticulously accurate in citations, frequently clairvoyant in interpreting a book or article, and scrupulously fair in summarizing or judging a work, they will likely have little notion of the quantity of work or the problems they will face in planning, researching, and writing their bibliographies. The common remark of one finishing a first bibliography is, "Now I know how to do a bibliography."

Hoping to forestall this reaction, contribute to the overall improvement of future bibliographies, and convince skeptics that annotated bibliography is an endeavor equivalent to "real" scholarship or criticism, I describe in the following pages procedures and techniques for compiling an annotated bibliography. Some of my suggestions will expand those of Colaianne; many will be obvious to readers. Although I focus on the preparation of a comprehensive annotated bibliography of scholarship on a single literary author and although many of my illustrations are from Renaissance literature, the procedures and techniques are easily adapted to selective[4] or subject bibliographies and to other periods and disciplines. While the compilation of an annotated bibliography must be an organized, orderly process, a compiler should not proceed in lockstep through the following outline. Constraints on time or on availability of material will frequently make it necessary to work concurrently on stages, and it is wise to alternate kinds of work—there is no surer road to bibliographical burnout than to do nothing for weeks on end but read sections of the *MLA International Bibliography*, the Modern Humanities Research Association *Annual Bibliography of English Language and Literature*, and *Dissertation Abstracts / Dissertation Abstracts International*.

Some Preliminaries

There are major questions you must ask before setting out to compile an annotated bibliography:

Is there a need for this bibliography?

You cannot merely decide that you will prepare a bibliography and then choose an author. Rather, you must establish, on the basis of a thorough knowledge of scholarship and reference works, that a bibliography would make an important contribution to the study of an author. There must be sufficient scholarship on and interest in the author—and any existing bibliography must be outdated or inadequate—to justify your investment of considerable time, energy, and (possibly) money.

Unless you can establish the importance of and audience for your work, you will likely not find a traditional publisher. Because of high publication costs, an increasingly discriminating (and dwindling) library market, and the preeminence of the Web over print as a medium for reference works, publishers are carefully evaluating market potential before issuing contracts for hard-copy bibliographies.[5] You should not begin a major bibliography without a contract or an agreement with a learned society or equivalent institution to sponsor and vet your work. Having a commitment from a publisher or the sponsorship of a learned society will increase your chances of obtaining clerical assistance, grant money, and released time for research.

Do I have the temperament and qualifications to do the work?

Above all, bibliographical research requires the infinite capacity for taking pains. You must be organized, accurate, thorough, and meticulous in your research. You must be willing to spend grueling hours (always more than you anticipate)[6] tracking down a partial or incorrect citation, searching carefully mounds of bibliographies and reference works, examining stacks of printouts from databases, composing hundreds of database entries, scanning library OPACs, filling out masses of interlibrary loan forms, and searching out and reading (in a variety of languages) piles of books, articles, and electronic documents, many of which will include nothing significant about the subject author. If you plan to publish electronically, you must have a reasonably sophisticated command of a good Web-authoring software package. You must patiently educate colleagues who look with condescension or disdain on your research. And, for your "chief reward," you must be satisfied with "the silent blessings of students and scholars down through the years" (Rollin 36).

Do I have the necessary resources to complete (and, with an electronic bibliography, maintain) the project?

Ideally, you will need a local library of about a million volumes to serve as a base, an efficient interlibrary loan service, and ready access to major research libraries. You cannot hope to compile an annotated bibliography by relying heavily on interlibrary loan: many books and periodicals will simply not be available for loan, and many libraries can no longer absorb the steadily escalating costs of interlibrary loan service. If your bibliography will be an electronic publication, you must provide continuous access.

5

You will incur expenses for travel (for extended periods if you are far from major research libraries) and possibly for photocopying, postage, research assistance, computer time, and keyboarding. Although most universities will underwrite a portion of these costs, funding is rarely sufficient to cover all expenses.[7] I know of no publisher who will pay an advance for a bibliography (since sales are limited), and prospective bibliographers should realize that they will not likely obtain grant support: several grant agencies and organizations (ironically, the Bibliographical Society of America) will not even accept proposals for annotated bibliographies.

Am I willing to publish updates and corrections?

Anyone who publishes a bibliography in electronic form must be committed to providing updated versions at regular intervals. Even authors of bibliographies published in hard copy have an obligation, in this electronic age, to offer periodic updates and corrections on the Web.

Organization of an Annotated Bibliography

The typical annotated bibliography (hard-copy version) consists of three parts: prefatory matter, entries, index. Since it can be searched by keyword and can offer hyperlinks, an electronic bibliography rarely includes an index. The content and organization of each part varies according to a publisher's established guidelines and the demands of the subject author or topic. To plan your research efficiently, you must establish the overall organization and content of each major section. Even if you are following a publisher's format, you should examine several existing bibliographies to familiarize yourself with how others have organized their works.[8]

Prefatory matter

Although most prefatory matter cannot be prepared until the entries are in final form, you should decide at the outset what you will include so that you can make notes, keep records, and draft portions as you work. This section typically consists of an introduction, an explanation of editorial procedures, acknowledgments, and separate lists of abbreviations, major reference sources searched, and the subject author's works. The statement of editorial procedures (which you must formulate before you begin your research) is essential, for it is here that a reader looks for an explanation of the scope, limitations, and organization of the bibliography. You must explain—and, if necessary, offer a rationale for—the taxonomy, the kinds of works included and excluded, and the chronological span (especially terminal date) of scholarship covered. You may also need to explain how you have dealt with problems in the subject author's canon, and you should establish the relation of your work to existing bibliographies.

Although the prefatory matter in many bibliographies is limited to a discussion of editorial procedures and a list of abbreviations, most readers appreciate an introductory essay that defines major trends in scholarship; identifies essential books, articles, and electronic documents; and suggests topics needing research. Such an introduction provides a perspective on and context for the mass of individual entries, should forestall a few superfluous discussions of overworked topics, and can influence productive new directions for research.

The prefatory matter must include a list of all abbreviations and acronyms that appear in citations and annotations; don't assume that readers will know even the commonest (e.g., OED, *STC*, *JEGP*, *MP*, *DNB*). In an electronic bibliography (where your publisher doesn't need to worry about paper cost) there is no excuse for using abbreviations and acronyms to save space. Although many bibliographers use acronyms when citing serial works (doing so can save time when preparing a lengthy manuscript), most readers prefer to have titles spelled out. Flipping continually to a list of acronyms is frustrating and time-consuming for a reader who is copying more than a few entries. If you do use acronyms, follow the Master List of Periodicals printed at the front of the current *MLA International Bibliography*, for it is the most familiar and widely used list of serial acronyms in language and literature. Since the Master List is not comprehensive and omits serials no longer published, you will have to invent some acronyms. If you do not use acronyms, maintain a checklist of serials you cite to ensure consistency in recording titles and to speed up the editing of entries. Watch carefully for changes in titles, and be aware that some periodicals use acronyms as titles (e.g., *PMLA* and *ELN*).

On Compiling an Annotated Bibliography

You should include a list of the subject author's works along with the corresponding short titles you use in annotations. (The list will also ensure consistency in the form and spelling of titles as you annotate studies.) Generally, you should avoid abbreviating titles of or using acronyms for the subject author's works; even the most familiar (e.g., *Ham.* for *Hamlet* or *PL* for *Paradise Lost*) will mystify some readers and detract from the readability of annotations.

Provide a list of bibliographies and other reference sources you have searched to let a reader judge the thoroughness of your research and identify other sources that must be checked. Also, this list will alert researchers to reference works that they may need to consult for studies published after your terminal date of coverage.

A good bibliography is a cooperative effort that involves fellow scholars, editors, research assistants, keyboarders, and librarians. Recognize individually those who made a substantial contribution to your work; thank others collectively. Avoid sentimentality and cuteness (e.g., forbear references to your favorite brand of scotch).

The entries

The citations and accompanying annotations are the heart of an annotated bibliography. How you organize this section will depend on a publisher's guidelines or the scholarship on the subject author or both. There are three basic ways of organizing entries: alphabetically by author, chronologically by date of publication, or topically by subject. The first is the least used these days, especially in lengthy bibliographies; its single advantage is that scholarly works by an important scholar are grouped together. Chronological arrangement is appropriate when scholarship has developed in defined stages or when it generally does not focus on particular works or topics; such an arrangement, like an alphabetical one, requires particularly careful and extensive subject indexing or hypertext linking.[9] A subject arrangement is appropriate when an author has written in several genres or when the scholarship generally focuses on individual works or distinct issues and topics. Such an organization usually requires sections for broad general studies; for biographical, bibliographical, thematic, and stylistic studies; and for individual works by the subject author. Effective subject organization requires careful establishment of mutually exclusive categories and should be kept as simple as possible; a too elaborate breakdown makes a bibliography difficult to use and requires a complicated cross-indexing system or excessive multiple listings.[10] You must determine early on the basic organization of your entries (especially if you use subject organization, which will necessitate multiple entries for some works) so that you can establish a filing system for your cards or a program for your computer. That even the most primitive electronic bibliography can be searched by keyword does not preclude the need for careful attention to the organization of entries. Many users will benefit more by being able to browse related entries (especially in a carefully thought-out subject taxonomy) than to rely on keyword or proximity searches.

The index

An otherwise fine print bibliography can be rendered virtually useless by a poorly conceived and produced index. The type of indexes will be determined by a publisher's guidelines, the organization of your entries, and the scholarship you cover. Although you cannot compile the indexes until entries are in final form, you should maintain a list of possible subject headings as you compose annotations. Keep in mind that subject headings should be unambiguous and should be composed with the user in mind.

On Compiling an Annotated Bibliography

Even though an index is unlikely to appear in an electronic bibliography, authors of electronic bibliographies can benefit from preparing traditional name and subject indexes; so doing will point up inconsistencies in forms of names and subject terms that can impede searching of electronic data. (For further discussion, see "Indexing.")

Planning Your Research

Producing a good bibliography—thorough, accurate, consistent, effectively organized, and efficiently indexed or hyperlinked—requires careful, systematic planning before you begin reading and annotating documents. In addition to determining the overall organization of your bibliography, you must accomplish four major tasks:

1. Reexamine thoroughly the subject author's life and works. As you reread all the primary texts and the major biographical and critical studies, compile a list of themes, figures, subjects, genres, forms, stylistic characteristics, sources, influences, biographical details, regions, and literary-historical topics associated with the subject author. In short, note anything that will help you determine what specialized bibliographies or reference works and what broad historical, thematic, or genre discussions you must read. (Alphabetize the list to use it as a convenient check when you search library catalogs, book indexes, or bibliographies. This list will also be useful when you are ready to formulate subject headings for the index.)

2. Decide what types of works you will include. Comprehensiveness—that elusive goal of a bibliographer—is possible only within carefully defined limits. A good bibliography includes all scholarship that researchers need but is not cluttered with inessential or repetitive entries. What you include will be determined by your intended audience, your publisher's requirements (including manuscript length restrictions for print bibliographies), and the scholarship you encounter. Since you will likely find it necessary to alter your inclusion policy as you read through the scholarship, begin with a broad rather than narrow one; otherwise, you will find yourself redoing much work.

On Compiling an Annotated Bibliography

In a comprehensive bibliography you should include all works that are wholly or substantially about the subject author. You should list, with appropriate annotations, studies that are decidedly wrongheaded, outrageous (e.g., an argument that Francis Bacon was the author of John Lyly's works), or superseded, to save your reader the trouble of tracking them down. However, if the subject author (e.g., Ralegh or More) has been the subject of numerous popular studies (e.g., articles in mass-circulation magazines, juvenile biographies, or historical romances), you should include only those that are in some way significant to the scholarly record. Don't omit a work because you have been unable to examine it; note your source for the entry and carefully distinguish whether you have been unable to examine, locate, or verify the work. Identifying ghosts that haunt other bibliographies will preclude fruitless searching by users.

You must also decide how you will treat revised or reprinted articles and books (including digitized reproductions or electronic versions), as well as extracts from books. A revised edition of a book or revised version of an article should receive a separate entry with an annotation indicating the nature of the revision. An article that is subsequently incorporated into a book should receive a separate entry, accompanied by a cross-reference to the book and an indication of the nature of the revision; the annotation for the book should also include a cross-reference to the article. An extract from a book or a reprint of an article (such as one finds frequently in collections of studies on an author) should at least be noted (as part of the original citation) for the convenience of the reader, since a reprint of an article in a collection is frequently more accessible than the original. A reprint of a book may also be included with the original citation; with few exceptions, listing separately every unrevised reprint of a book merely wastes space.[11]

Although you should include reviews of books by the subject author, you will need to decide whether to include reviews of books wholly or substantially about the subject author. Reviews that are significant critical discussions or that offer substantial corrections or additions should generally receive separate entries; citations to other reviews may simply be appended to appropriate annotations.

Some recent bibliographies have omitted PhD dissertations or have relegated them, unannotated, to an appendix. While it is appropriate to omit masters' theses (few offer truly significant contributions, and they are particularly difficult to obtain and are not abstracted with any consistency), excluding doctoral dissertations undermines the value of a bibliography.[12] Much significant research is available only in unpublished dissertations; omitting these works distorts the record of scholarship in a bibliography. And remember that graduate students in search of dissertation topics are among the most devoted readers of bibliographies.

Excluding scholarship in languages other than English also distorts the record of scholarship and undermines the usefulness of a bibliography. Scholarship on almost every author is international in scope; thus you will need a good reading knowledge of languages in which scholarship on the subject author is concentrated. (Enlist colleagues or translators for help with languages you do not know.) Securing foreign publications—except for those in a non-Latin alphabet or published in Asia or South America—is not as difficult as it might seem.

Because anyone with access to a server can "publish" documents on the Web, you will likely encounter numerous Web sites or Web pages devoted to your author. You should generally include (with a hyperlink) only those that conform to the "Minimal Guidelines for Authors of Web Pages" (formulated by the MLA's Committee on Computers and Emerging Technologies in Teaching and Research), that have undergone some kind of vetting, and that are sponsored by a reputable institution, learned society, or agency.

Works that also pose difficult decisions are the broad-ranging literary histories, encyclopedias, and studies of a theme, genre, or movement that include a brief discussion of the subject author. If, in your estimation, a brief discussion is in some way significant—for example, if it offers new facts or interpretations or has been particularly influential—then include it. Otherwise, resist cluttering your bibliography with scores of entries for plot summaries or perfunctory rehashes of critical or biographical commonplaces.

Anthologies also prove troublesome. While you should include critical editions of the subject author's works, listing every anthology appearance of a popular poem, short story, or play needlessly swells the number of entries, diverts a reader's attention from the important scholarship, and consumes an inordinate amount of research time. Of course, make exceptions for appearances in particularly influential anthologies or those that include significant critical or textual commentary.

Deciding when to include allusions to the subject author in a poem or other creative work is another problem you might face. You might include allusions that have significantly influenced subsequent critical opinion (e.g., Jonson's "To the Memory of My Beloved, the Author, Mr. William Shakespeare: And What He Hath Left Us"); omit the remainder, especially when a good reception study of the author exists.

3. Announce your bibliography in appropriate scholarly journals and electronic forums. (For journals, do this as early as possible since the content of issues is usually fixed far in advance of publication.) Announcements will

encourage scholars to send offprints, information on little-known works, or notices of publications in press.

4. Choose a good style manual—if your publisher doesn't provide or specify one—and thoroughly familiarize yourself with it before you begin preparing entries.[13] You can save considerable time by knowing citation form for—and how to recognize—various kinds of publications (e.g., books in a series, separately titled volumes in collected works, journals that paginate separately issues within a volume), capitalization rules for foreign languages, and other conventions of form and style. (This knowledge is essential even if you use a word-processing or bibliography program with built-in style manuals: computer programs merely format entries; you must know what to input.) Be certain to review frequently the style manual and publisher's guidelines. (If you use a software program that reformats electronic records downloaded from OPACs, union catalogs, or databases, be certain that you check these records against the actual documents before transferring them to your electronic manuscript.) An author's failure to follow required citation style or format is one of the commonest reasons for delay in publication of a bibliography: the manuscript must be either extensively revised by the author or copyedited by the publisher.

Compiling the Entries

There are three major steps to compiling the entries: identifying scholarly works, obtaining them, and writing the entries. To achieve comprehensiveness within the limitations you have established, you must be thorough in your research. To proceed efficiently and systematically, establish a filing system to record works identified, located, annotated, or rejected. For example, before laptop computers were available, I used two complementary files. I maintained an alphabetized master file of 3" × 5" cards recording every work that I had identified, located, ordered from a publisher or through interlibrary loan, requested an offprint of, queried an author about, failed to verify or locate, annotated, or read and rejected. To mark the status of each card, I used colored metal tabs (available from any office-supply store). I consulted this file when searching bibliographies or footnotes and thus avoided recording or tracking down the same book, article, or dissertation a half dozen different times; I packed along the file boxes—or conveniently extracted appropriate cards—when visiting another library; I could immediately determine how much and what kind of work I had yet to do; I had a record of call number and location if I had to reexamine a work. I maintained a second file—corresponding to the organization of the bibliography—of completed entries. (Although I used a computer for compiling the entries, I still maintained a file of typed entries for security.) Now, however, I've replaced the card files with a laptop and database. Whatever system you develop, you must have some clear, orderly, and convenient way of keeping track of your work.

Identifying scholarly works

Identifying scholarly works involves much more than conflating the listings of three or four major bibliographies (those who classify annotated bibliography as clerical drudgery frequently think bibliographers do nothing else). You must first survey existing bibliographies and reference works to identify those you will have to check thoroughly. These will include not only the obvious ones (e.g., *MLA International Bibliography*, Modern Humanities Research Association *Annual Bibliography of English Language and Literature*, *New Cambridge Bibliography of English Literature*, *Year's Work in Modern Language Studies*, *Bulletin signalétique 523*, or *Internationale Bibliographie der Zeitschriftenliteratur*) but also specialized bibliographies covering particular kinds of publications or focusing on periods, authors, genres, subjects, or themes that are pertinent to your subject author.[14]

Establish the order in which you will search the reference works you have identified. Begin with published bibliographies on the subject author, then go to the general serial bibliographies and databases, then to period bibliographies, and finish with the bibliographies on themes, genres, types of publications, and so on.

You should also identify journals and Web sites that are devoted to the subject author and to his or her period or that have published a significant number of articles on the subject author; journals should be checked volume by volume (along with any cumulative indexes).[15] Maintain a careful record of reference works, Web sites, and journals you have searched.

Your next step is to begin accumulating a file on works you must obtain and read. After identifying reference sources and determining the order in which you will search them, you must check each thoroughly, sometimes scanning every entry (even in databases).[16] Before copying any entries from a reference work, familiarize yourself with its organization, scope, comprehensiveness, and index (and, in databases, search strategies and access points). (Remember that scope, organization, and indexing procedures sometimes change radically in serial or multivolume works published over several years.) Only by examining the organization of a work in relation to your list of topics associated with the subject author can you determine how to search a particular reference work.

The *MLA International Bibliography*, which has undergone major changes in scope and taxonomy, effectively illustrates the need to become thoroughly familiar with a reference work.[17] For example, before 1956 the *Bibliography* nominally included works by American scholars only. Although it became "international" in 1956, it is still not exhaustive in its coverage. The taxonomy and indexing procedures have also changed, most radically with the *Bibliography* for 1981, which introduced a sophisticated classification and indexing system.[18] In searching the *MLA International Bibliography*, you would, of course, examine the entries in the subject-author section (and, for post-1980 volumes, the subject-author listings in the comprehensive subject index). In addition, you would have to search (1) the General heading and relevant genre headings in appropriate period sections (in the 1981 *Bibliography* and after, you cannot follow this procedure, because general studies of a theme or genre in a single national literature are listed according to chronological span covered—e.g., a study of the English lyric from 1300 to 1900 would be listed under "English Literature/ 1300–1899" and would appear near the beginning of the English section of volume 1); (2) the English I (General and Miscellaneous) and English III (Themes, Types, and Special Topics) sections or the American I (General and Miscellaneous) section; (3) possibly all of the following sections, depending on the year of the *Bibliography*: General I (Esthetics), General II (Literary Criticism and Literary Theory), General III (Literature, General and Comparative), General IV (Themes and Types), General V (Bibliographical), and General VI (Miscellaneous). (In the 1981 *Bibliography* and after, the General headings of volume 1 have been replaced by volume 4 [General Literature and Related Topics], which now includes the following main divisions: General Literature, Dramatic Arts, Literary Movements, Bibliographical, Literary Theory and Criticism, Genres, Figures of Speech, Literary Forms, Professional Topics, and Themes and Figures. Since cross-references are no longer used, it is imperative that you also check all relevant topics on your list in the comprehensive subject index, not the index to an individual volume.)

Only after becoming thoroughly familiar with a reference source should you begin copying entries from it. You can save time by downloading entries from a database or marking printouts or photocopies of pages for a keyboarder to input from. However you proceed, be certain to expand acronyms or abbreviations (especially for journal titles), copy an entry completely and accurately, add diacritics and italics to printouts from databases, and note precisely the source (including, where appropriate, year, volume, page, and entry number). Recording this information fully will save you from having to relocate an entry to complete an interlibrary loan request (which requires complete publication information and verification in a source) or will allow you to check for possible transcription errors in a citation for a book or article you cannot locate.

Of course, you will find that the reference sources you check will overlap—sometimes considerably—yet each, because of its respective purpose, scope, or organization, will include works listed in none of the others or will bring to your attention books or articles that you overlooked in other sources. (For example, not all articles abstracted in *Abstracts of English Studies* or indexed in *Arts and Humanities Citation Index* will be listed in the *MLA International Bibliography*, and the abstracts and index in the first and the subject and citation indexes in the second will lead you to articles overlooked in your search of the *MLA International Bibliography*.) The reference sources you search will not identify every work pertinent to your subject author. You will need to supplement your search of standard sources by examining footnotes and bibliographies in the books and articles you read; publishers' catalogs; reviews, lists of books received, and journal contents lists in scholarly periodicals; appropriate Dewey and Library of Congress ranges; and trade or national bibliographies such as *American Book Publishing Record*, *British National Bibliography*, and *Livres du mois*.

As you search these various sources, consult your master file continually so that you do not waste time and effort by duplicating cards.

In your research you will encounter a number of vague, ambiguous, or downright uninformative titles of works that may discuss your subject author. (By knowing thoroughly the subject author you will develop the bibliographer's sixth sense about these frustrating titles.) Record and examine such works, for a surprising number will prove worthy of inclusion in your bibliography.

Searching all the necessary sources to identify pertinent books, dissertations, and articles will be time-consuming, tedious, and wearying. To reduce the mental fatigue that arises from such a repetitive task, you should alternate identifying, locating, reading, and annotating works.

Obtaining works

As soon as you accumulate a file of two to three hundred records, you should begin locating copies. Many will be available in your own university library (recall my earlier stricture that you need a collection of about one million volumes to serve as an adequate base for your research); others will require travel to nearby major research libraries; some will be available through interlibrary loan or through reprint services;[19] and some will require correspondence with authors, publishers, scholars, or libraries.

Public access to library networks such as OCLC or RLIN has made it easier for researchers to identify frustratingly incomplete references and to determine which libraries own a particular work (and edition thereof).[20] Still, you will have to pore over volumes of the *National Union Catalog: Pre-1956 Imprints*, *National Union Catalog*, *Union List of Serials*, *New Serial Titles*, and the OPACs of individual libraries (such as the British Library or Library of Congress) to locate elusive works.[21] Sort into groups the records for titles available in nearby libraries until you have a sufficient number to justify a trip. Works you must obtain through interlibrary loan should be requested as early as possible in your research: there are sometimes delays in borrowing items, and some will not be available for loan.

You can secure copies of works unavailable in libraries you visit or through interlibrary loan—if you allow adequate time. In other words, don't wait until you have located everything else to begin searching for the difficult-to-find items. To obtain such works, try these strategies:

a. Write directly to the publisher. Books and issues of journals published years ago may still be in print even though they are not recorded in standard sources such as *Books in Print*.

b. Post a list of books wanted with Web search engines that scour antiquarian and out-of-print book sites.

c. Purchase from the holding library a microfilm or photocopy of a work too fragile or rare to be loaned.

d. Write to other scholars who have cited the work. You can frequently obtain a photocopy, a summary, or at least information about or location of a copy.

e. Request an offprint of an article from the author (and inquire whether he or she has published other works you may not be aware of). The following are useful sources of addresses: the annual Directory issue of *PMLA* (and directories published by specialized journals and organizations), *National Faculty Directory*, *World of Learning*, *Commonwealth Universities Yearbook*, *World Guide to Universities*, people-search features of Web search engines, and *Arts and Humanities Citation Index*.

f. Write to the library of the sponsoring institution or organization regarding a limited-circulation publication. This is frequently the best way to obtain a copy of an article from a journal no longer published or of restricted circulation.

When tracking down an elusive work, note on its record all the places and sources you have searched so that you can avoid retracing your steps.

Obtaining dissertations poses special problems. Since acquiring a copy of every possibly relevant unpublished dissertation—especially those submitted to universities outside the United States—is prohibitively expensive and ultimately impossible, you must frequently be content to work from summaries.[22] Even after combing *Dissertation Abstracts International* (and its predecessors), volumes of summaries published by individual universities, separately published abstracts, and journals that regularly publish(ed) summaries, you will be unable to locate abstracts of many dissertations.[23] For these, write the author, requesting a photocopy of any abstract or a brief summary. (I have found that most authors will gladly comply, and many are flattered to discover that someone is actually interested in their dissertations.) If you cannot locate an author, ask the head of the department that accepted the dissertation whether there is a file copy from which a summary might be photocopied, or write the library of the granting institution to request a photocopy of any abstract in the deposit copy. Be aware, however, that purchasing copies of more than a few abstracts will be costly since most libraries impose a minimum per item photocopying charge.

Writing the entries

As soon as you obtain a few works, begin preparing entries. By doing so you will avoid the tedium of repeating a single process, identify other works that you need to examine, and isolate problems that you will need to consult your editor about. But before you actually write an entry, you must deal with some preliminaries:

a. Become thoroughly familiar with your style manual. Knowing the citation form for various kinds of publications (especially books in series, volumes of collected works, and periodicals published in series or as separate issues not collected in numbered volumes) will allow you to record all pertinent information from a work in hand and thus preclude the need to reexamine it at the editing stage.

b. Establish your taxonomy. This step is especially important if you will use a subject arrangement or prepare your manuscript with the aid of a database program. In a subject arrangement, you may want to enter a work under several subject headings, with a different annotation each time; if you alter your taxonomy after preparing such multiple entries, you may have to return to the work and write new annotations. If you plan to use a database program, you must give careful attention to the design of a system and format for entering records.[24] You must determine how you want to sort and retrieve entries before you type in the first one. (See the section "Using a Computer to Prepare Your Manuscript," p. 30.)

c. Decide what kind of annotations you will write. The type (paraphrase or commentary), approach (degree of evaluation), and style of your annotations will be determined by a publisher's guidelines, the demands of the scholarship you cover, and personal preference. You should, of course, survey some good published bibliographies for examples (see note 8).

It is important to decide at the outset between the paraphrase and commentary approach to annotations. As Willis J. Buckingham astutely observes:

> Paraphrase takes the point of view of the item it abstracts; following its sequence of ideas, it provides a miniaturized transcription of the original. Commentary speaks from its own, usually disinterested perspective about the major concerns of the work cited and its approach to them. While in commentary there may be description of the author's argument, there is no necessary attempt at faithful reproduction of it. The commentary annotator serves the scholarly researcher as an expert indexer. He prepares his annotation with a sense that the likely user of his listing will be more concerned with what it is about than in what it says, so as to determine quickly whether it is worth examining in the original. Given skill and knowledge, an annotator can provide that information, even for an entire book-length study, in a few crisp and pointed sentences.
>
> The summary annotator, on the other hand, primarily serves his reader as a redactor. His purpose is at once to transcribe and reduce the scale of a body of documents surrounding a particular subject. For this task he needs skills of verbal compression but by comparison with commentary, summary is properly more spacious and leisured. Like a shadow, the precis

delineates the substance of the body that casts it. An inflated argument, of course, can be paraphrased more quickly than an incisive one. That variable aside, one expects the length of an abstract to bear some proportion to its original. (203–04)

The following examples will serve to illustrate the differences between the two types. The first is a paraphrase annotation by Mary A. Washington (112):

> 514. ENDICOTT, ANNABEL. "Pip, Philip and Astrophel: Dickens' Debt to Sidney?" *Dickensian*, 63 (1966), 158–62.
> Sidney was the inspiration of Dickens' concept of a gentleman as given in *Great Expectations*. Philip and Estella have parallels with Philip and Stella. Both Philips love married women of higher rank; both have friends who try to dissuade them. The words "great expectations" occur in Sonnet 21. Dickens may have been exploring the idea of the Petrarchan convention; certainly Estella resembles the Petrarchan mistress.

In commentary form, the annotation might read: "Suggests *Astrophil and Stella* as the source of Dickens's concept of a gentleman and exploration of Petrarchan convention in *Great Expectations*."

The second example is a commentary annotation by John R. Roberts (*George Herbert* 226):

> 706. JOHNSON, LEE ANN. "The Relationship of 'The Church Militant' to *The Temple*." SP 68:200–206.
> Surveys attempts of various modern critics to explain the exact relationship of *The Church Militant* to the total design of *The Temple* and finds all of them unconvincing. Maintains that the content and the formal and stylistic characteristics of *The Church Militant* and especially its positioning in the early folios suggest that it should be considered as a separate entity and not as an organic part of the three-part structure of *The Temple*.

Of course, it is impossible to be completely objective in writing annotations. Your choice of words (e.g., saying that a scholar "asserts" rather than "proves" or "establishes") conveys your judgment of a work; through judicious quotation, you can easily allow an author to condemn himself or herself. What you do need to decide is how overt your evaluation will be. For example, a few bibliographers use symbols (commonly an asterisk or star) to identify important studies. Such an approach should be accompanied by annotations that clearly specify the importance of works; merely tagging something as "seminal," "definitive," or "outstanding" is not particularly informative. Finally, the quality and significance of a study—not your critical biases—must be the bases for evaluation; annotations that reflect prejudice against a particular methodology, critical theory, or type of scholarship breed distrust in users.

You must also establish your annotation style. Decide on tense (historical present is most commonly used) and voice (avoid passive, if at all possible), and, as Colaianne advises, "take advantage [in commentary annotations] of the connotations of 'annotation verbs'" such as "demonstrates," "asserts," "speculates," "supposes," and "proves" (328–29). (Don't overuse the flat ones such as "discusses" and "examines"; see the appendix on p. 45.) Annotations should be readable: paraphrase annotations should be composed of complete sentences; in commentary annotations, subjectless sentences ("Argues that . . ." or "Transcribes Keats's marginalia . . .") are acceptable. But omitting articles, prepositions, and the like reduces the readability of an annotation.

Whatever approach you adopt, be consistent throughout your annotations. Don't mix paraphrase and commentary, and don't switch voice or tense within or between citations. Inconsistency is disconcerting to someone reading more than a few entries.

In composing annotations (especially paraphrase ones), maintain a sense of proportion. While the length of an annotation need not always reflect the significance or length of a work, short articles should not consistently be accorded as many or more words as a major book. (Of course, some books can be more succinctly annotated than many articles.)

Whether paraphrase or commentary, good annotations accurately and incisively—but not cryptically—distill the essence of works. Or, as Arthur Kinney says, they "pierce to the heart of the matter; [. . .] isolate what is new; [. . .] make clear the presuppositions, premises, and prejudices of the material and of its author; [. . .] highlight what is distinctive and new; and [. . . are] phrased in a way that makes them useful for both the specialist [. . .] and the nonspecialist" (174). Good annotations focus the reader's attention on major points and do not attempt to recapitulate every step of a process, note every piece of evidence, trace every digression, or account for every passing comment.

To accomplish this ideal requires critical acumen and a thorough familiarity with the development of and crosscurrents in scholarship on the subject author. Therefore, you should annotate first the major scholarly works; doing so will provide a context in which to annotate the bulk of entries.

Composing an accurate annotation requires that you read the work (unless, of course, you must rely on an abstract for a dissertation). A work is frequently more—or less—than an author announces; some works will lack a thesis altogether. By reading the introductory and concluding sections and skimming the remainder, you risk producing a misleading or incomplete annotation.

Immediately after reading a work, compose a "finished" entry, enter it into your computer, proofread it while the work is in hand,[25] note any odd spellings or other peculiarities that might evoke a copyeditor's query, and store it to await the final editing stage. Merely accumulating notes that you plan eventually to turn into entries will result in having to reexamine many works: notes that seem clear immediately after reading a study are impossibly cryptic two or three months later, especially after you have read three to four hundred related books and articles in the interim.

Once you have composed a hundred or so entries, you should pause to review citation form (review your style manual once again) and to evaluate your taxonomy and annotation style, especially for consistency, clarity, and succinctness. Almost invariably your early annotations will be wordy and, when read as a group, stylistically inconsistent. After making necessary revisions, you should send a copy of these entries to your editor, who can alert you to any problems, and you should ask a few trusted colleagues to evaluate your work. The more problems you can correct at this early stage, the easier and quicker your final editing will be.

Using a Computer to Prepare Your Manuscript

The few hours you devote to mastering a sophisticated word-processing program will be amply compensated by the weeks you will save in arranging, proofreading, editing, and indexing entries and in printing a final manuscript.

Using a computer, you can prepare your manuscript (including much of the index) as you compose the entries instead of waiting until you have finished them all. After typing in an entry, you can index, edit, sort, retrieve, and print it (along with others) at will. When you have completed the final editing, you will be able to produce both printed and electronic copies of your manuscript.[26]

Final Editing

After you have finished all the entries, you will need to edit your work before preparing a final copy and (for a print bibliography) index. In addition to proofreading carefully, you must do the following (in order):

a. Review entries for consistency with your editorial policy. In particular, check for works of types that your policy excludes and for consistency in handling revisions and reprints—in short, make sure that what you include is consistent with the scope and limitations of your coverage.

b. Check annotations for consistency in type and style. Be sure that you have used the same type of annotation throughout and that entries are consistent in voice and tense. At this point, you should also standardize—except in quotations—the form and spelling of names, terms, and titles throughout the annotations. As you check entries, compile an alphabetized checklist as a guide; don't rely on your memory.

c. Recheck citation form against your style manual. In particular, be sure that you use the same form of an author's name throughout (expand names within square brackets—e.g., if you cite Muriel Clara Bradbrook, then Muriel C. Bradbrook and M. C. Bradbrook should appear, respectively, as Muriel C[lara] Bradbrook and M[uriel] C[lara] Bradbrook). Also, compile the final list of acronyms and abbreviations as you check citation form; use the list to ensure consistency among entries.

d. Review your taxonomy and be sure that entries are in proper order.

e. Number entries. Keep the numbering system as simple as possible since the index will be keyed to entry numbers.

f. After numbering entries, add the necessary cross-references or hyperlinks for such things as direct rebuttals, reviews, additions, revisions, reprints, supplements; otherwise, use cross-references or hyperlinks sparingly. To trace every strand of every topic of scholarship will produce a confusing, if not unreadable, entry.

Indexing

After the final editing, you are ready to index the entries. If you are preparing an electronic bibliography, creating a traditional index—even though you won't include it—will reveal inconsistencies in personal names and subject terms; consistency is important if keyword searches are to locate all entries by a document author or about a subject. Whether you prepare your index by computer or file cards, you must have a clear understanding of indexing principles and techniques. Before you begin, study carefully a detailed guide to indexing (e.g., *Chicago Manual* 701–61 or Knight) and examine the indexes of some published bibliographies.[27]

As you plan your index, keep foremost in mind the needs of researchers, the majority of whom will consult your bibliography to identify quickly and easily studies by a particular scholar or on a specific work or topic. Providing entries for proper names and titles, whether in citations or annotations, is straightforward. Creating subject headings and subheadings is more demanding, for terms must "be clear, concise, logical, and consistent throughout" (*Chicago Manual* 731). (Examples of subject headings and subheadings that might be appropriate include bibliography, biography, characterization, humor, influence [followed by appropriate authors], imagery, language, setting, sources [followed by appropriate authors], structure, style, themes [followed by appropriate specific themes such as death, justice, and memory].) Since a good index must be thorough and clear, you must allow sufficient time to think through and compile entries. An otherwise fine bibliography can be rendered nearly useless by inadequate indexing.

Writing the Prefatory Matter

Once you have finished the final editing and indexing, you will be ready to compose the prefatory material. (See "Prefatory matter," pp. 7–9.) If you have kept careful notes during the research and writing of the entries, this work will go quickly. Specifically, you must (1) prepare the final version of your editorial policy (being careful to incorporate changes you made during the course of your research) and other introductory material, (2) proofread the list of acronyms and abbreviations you compiled as you checked for consistency in citation style, (3) compile the list of bibliographies and other reference sources you searched, (4) recheck the list of the subject author's works, and (5) acknowledge those who made a significant contribution to your work. Finally, compose a brief note requesting that users report (inevitable) omissions or new studies for incorporation in the supplement you have already begun.

Concluding Remarks

Despite the prescriptive tone of many of my remarks, what I have outlined is a flexible procedure. You will need to modify or rearrange steps to accord with your own work habits and the demands of your subject. Merely attending to the mechanics of the process will not ensure a bibliography that is a thorough, accurate, and usable contribution to scholarship. To achieve this aim, you must add the determination, meticulousness, energy, time, critical acumen, and literary detective skills that one associates with the best scholarship of any kind.

Notes

[1] I am grateful to the following bibliographers for their helpful comments: Harrison T. Meserole, Jerome S. Dees, Brownell Salomon, John R. Roberts, Paul Klemp, Larry S. Champion, James S. Dean, William Miller, Walter Scheps, Willard Fox, Elizabeth Hageman, Greg Beene, Tim Conley, D. Jerry White, and Sara Jayne Steen.

[2] For example, see Meserole, "A Bibliographer's *Apologia pro vita sua.*"

[3] In particular, see Buckingham and Kinney.

[4] The assumption that a selective bibliography is easier than a comprehensive bibliography to research and write is erroneous. Principles of selection must be carefully established in terms of an intended audience. Too often selectivity merely reflects what a compiler was able to locate in the stacks of a sizable library and in a hasty perusal of a few major reference works.

[5] To identify publishers interested in bibliographies, consult Harner, *MLA Directory of Scholarly Presses.*

There are alternatives to commercial book publication, especially in journals. For example, *Bulletin of Bibliography* and *English Literature in Transition* print bibliographies, *English Literary Renaissance* regularly includes essay reviews of scholarship, and *Resources for American Literary Study* publishes updates of book-length bibliographies. (For other journals that publish bibliographies, see the current edition of *MLA Directory of Periodicals.*)

[6] A common myth is that an annotated bibliography is a quick book, the kind of publication ideally suited to filling up a curriculum vitae in the scramble for promotion or tenure. While a shoddy bibliography—like a shoddy book of any kind—can be churned out quickly, a good bibliography requires time.

[7] Keep a careful record of all unreimbursed expenses for income-tax purposes.

[8] Some bibliographies that have been well received by reviewers and are useful as examples include Roberts, *John Donne* and *George Herbert*; Harner, *World Shakespeare Bibliography on CD-ROM 1900–Present*; Fox; Harner, *English Renaissance Prose Fiction*; Gerber and Davis; Giantvalley; and Champion.

On Compiling an Annotated Bibliography

Currently, the best Web-based bibliographies are commercial ones (such as the *MLA International Bibliography* or *The World Shakespeare Bibliography*). Because we are in a transition period between print and electronic bibliographies, most of those available free on the Web are little more than digitized print versions. However, the *Internet Movie Database* (currently free) is an excellent example of how bibliographers can exploit the capabilities of the Web.

[9] Since a chronological organization emphasizes the development of scholarly or critical opinion, enter published works by date of first publication, dissertations by date of acceptance, and unpublished works (e.g., letters or unpublished conference papers) by date of composition or delivery. Enter a revised book or article under the publication date of the revision. Never list a work under the date of a reprint because you have been unable to examine the original edition. (Apparently assuming that the publication of a reprint automatically reflects the growth of an author's reputation, some bibliographers enter reprints, especially of books, under the year of reprinting. This practice distorts the record of development of scholarship and usually does more to chronicle the vagaries of the publishing industry than to trace an author's reputation. For exceptions in a bibliography of a major author or a serial bibliography, see note 11.) See "Planning Your Research," section 2, for further discussion of reprints of books and articles.

[10] For an example of subject organization, see a recent issue of Harner, "Shakespeare: Annotated World Bibliography."

[11] The user's need for information about reprinted essays is obvious. For example, no library cataloging system will identify the numerous reprintings (under various titles) of T. S. Eliot's introduction to *Seneca His Tenne Tragedies Translated into English*. A user searching for a book, however, can readily identify a library's holdings of an original edition and reprints.

Reprints of books—at least those wholly or substantially about the subject author—may justifiably be given separate entries in bibliographies of major authors, wherein reprints can be valuable indications of an author's reputation, or in serial bibliographies, whose intent is to record all that was published about an author in a given year.

[12] A dissertation that is subsequently published should receive a separate entry, with a cross-reference to the book or article and—if possible—an indication of the nature of the revision; the annotation for the book or article should also provide a cross-reference to the dissertation.

On Compiling an Annotated Bibliography

[13] Most publishers follow *The Chicago Manual of Style*; Gibaldi, *MLA Style Manual*; or Gibaldi, *MLA Handbook*. If your bibliography will be accessible in a data bank, follow the citation style of the American National Standards Institute (*American National Standard for Bibliographic References*).

[14] In compiling a preliminary list of bibliographies and reference works, consult Harner, *Literary Research Guide*; Marcuse; and Balay. For example, I recommend that a bibliographer working on a Renaissance author check the following:

Serial bibliographies
MLA International Bibliography
Modern Humanities Research Association *Annual Bibliography of English Language and Literature*
Essay and General Literature Index
Humanities Index (formerly *Social Sciences and Humanities Index*)
British Humanities Index (formerly *Subject Index to Periodicals*)
Nineteenth Century Readers' Guide to Periodical Literature
Readers' Guide to Periodical Literature
Year's Work in English Studies
Annual Magazine and Subject Index (formerly *Annual Literary Index*, *Annual Library Index*, and *Cooperative Index to Periodicals*)
Abstracts of English Studies
English and American Studies in German: Summaries of Theses and Monographs (supplements to *Anglia*)
Arts and Humanities Citation Index (and *Current Contents*)
Internationale Bibliographie der Zeitschriftenliteratur
Index to Social Sciences and Humanities Proceedings
Bulletin signalétique 523: Histoire et sciences de la littérature

Period bibliographies
New Cambridge Bibliography of English Literature, vol. 1
Cambridge Bibliography of English Literature, vol. 1 (and supplement)
"Literature of the Renaissance" in *Studies in Philology*, 1917–69
Renaissance Bulletin (Tokyo) (each number from 1974 through 1984 includes a bibliography of studies published in Japan)
Bibliographie internationale de l'Humanisme et de la Renaissance
Hans Walter Gabler, *English Renaissance Studies in German, 1945–1967*

On Compiling an Annotated Bibliography

Author bibliographies

Samuel A. Tannenbaum, *Elizabethan Bibliographies*

Elizabethan Bibliographies Supplements (by various authors)

Terence P. Logan and Denzell S. Smith, eds., *The Predecessors of Shakespeare*; *The Popular School*; *The New Intellectuals*; *The Later Jacobean and Caroline Dramatists*

Shakespeare Association Bulletin (each volume prints a bibliography by Tannenbaum that includes several items not in his *Elizabethan Bibliographies*)

Walther Ebisch and Levin I. Schücking, *A Shakespeare Bibliography* (and supplement)

Gordon Ross Smith, *A Classified Shakespeare Bibliography, 1936–1958*

James L. Harner, ed., "Shakespeare: Annotated World Bibliography" (annually in *Shakespeare Quarterly*)

James L. Harner, *World Shakespeare Bibliography on CD-ROM 1900–Present.*

Shakespeare Jahrbuch (annual bibliography in both Heidelberg and Weimar publications)

Dissertation bibliographies

Comprehensive Dissertation Index

Dissertation Abstracts International

Index to Theses with Abstracts Accepted for Higher Degrees by the Universities of Great Britain and Ireland

Lawrence F. McNamee, *Dissertations in English and American Literature* (and supplements)

Roger R. Bilboul, cd., *Retrospective Index to Theses of Great Britain and Ireland, 1716–1950*, vol. 1, *Social Sciences and Humanities*

Gernot U. Gabel and Gisela R. Gabel, *Dissertations in English and American Literature: Theses Accepted by Austrian, French, and Swiss Universities, 1875–1970* (and supplement) and *Catalogue of Austrian and Swiss Dissertations (1875–1995) on English and American Literature*

Richard Mummendey, *Language and Literature of the Anglo-Saxon Nations as Presented in German Doctoral Dissertations, 1885–1950*

Michael M. Reynolds, *A Guide to Theses and Dissertations: An International Bibliography of Bibliographies*

Miscellaneous bibliographies

Fernand Baldensperger and Werner P. Friederich, *Bibliography of Comparative Literature*

Jacek Fisiak, ed., *Bibliografia anglistyki polskiej, 1945–1975 / Bibliography of Writings on English Language and Literature in Poland, 1945–1975*

E. L. C. Mullins, *Guide to the Historical and Archaeological Publications of Societies in England and Wales, 1901–1933* (continued by *Writings on British History* and *Annual Bibliography of British and Irish History*)

Arnold N. Rzepecki, *Literature and Language Bibliographies from the American Yearbook, 1910–1919*

T. H. Howard-Hill, *Index to British Literary Bibliography*

Dictionary of National Biography

OCLC

RLIN

National Union Catalog: Pre-1956 Imprints

National Union Catalog

[15] To identify appropriate journals, consult the current edition of the *MLA Directory of Periodicals*, Patterson, and Bracken. The best meta-pages for locating literature-related sites on the Web are *Literary Resources on the Net* and *Voice of the Shuttle*.

[16] Computer searches of databases such as the *MLA International Bibliography*, Modern Humanities Research Association *Annual Bibliography of English Language and Literature*, and *Dissertation Abstracts International* will identify works that are wholly or substantially devoted to an author, but only a close scrutiny of their print versions will reveal all the general studies that might discuss your author.

[17] For a fuller description of changes in the organization and scope of the *MLA International Bibliography*, see Harner, *Literary Research Guide* 47–51.

[18] Read carefully the "Guide for Users" at the front of the current volume.

[19] Maintain a file of photocopies of works obtained through interlibrary loan, or at the least record the location of every work you borrow in case you must recheck something.

[20] An author search of OCLC or RLIN records is a useful way to identify books possibly related to one that is relevant to your bibliog-

raphy. Despite their scope, OCLC and RLIN do not supersede the *National Union Catalog: Pre-1956 Imprints*, especially for works published before 1900.

[21] Most libraries now allow public access through computer networks to their online catalogs.

[22] If your university library is a member of the Center for Research Libraries, the center will attempt to purchase a copy of a foreign dissertation and loan it to you.

[23] See Reynolds for a convenient guide to bibliographies of dissertations.

[24] A useful discussion of the need for and process of system design appears in Oakman 97–110. For an extended example, see Meserole and Smith, "'Yet there is method in it.'"

[25] Ideally, someone else should proofread the entry; we all tend to repeat errors when proofreading our own work. Proofread diligently; it takes only a few careless errors to render an entire bibliography suspect.

[26] Publishers that accept electronic manuscripts will supply authors with information on special coding and acceptable operating systems and programs. Walker is the best general guide to preparing electronic manuscripts.

[27] Petry (65–70) discusses shortcomings of indexing in some recent bibliographies.

Works Cited

(Note: Omitted here are journals and reference works referred to in passing and in the list in note 14.)

American National Standards Institute. *American National Standard for Bibliographic References*. New York: Amer. Natl. Standards Inst., 1977. (ANSI Document no. Z39.29-1977.)

Balay, Robert, ed. *Guide to Reference Books*. 11th ed. Chicago: Amer. Lib. Assn., 1996.

Bracken, James K. *Reference Works in British and American Literature*. 2nd ed. Reference Sources in the Humanities. Englewood: Libraries Unlimited, 1998.

Buckingham, Willis J. "The G. K. Hall Reference Guides in Literature Series: An Essay Review." *Resources for American Literary Study* 8 (1978): 200–10.

Champion, Larry S. King Lear: *An Annotated Bibliography*. 2 vols. Garland Reference Library of the Humanities 230: Garland Shakespeare Bibliographies 1. New York: Garland, 1980.

The Chicago Manual of Style. 14th ed. Chicago: U of Chicago P, 1993.

Colaianne, A. J. "The Aims and Methods of Annotated Bibliography." *Scholarly Publishing* 11 (1980): 321–31.

Committee on Computers and Emerging Technologies in Teaching and Research. "Minimal Guidelines for Authors of Web Pages." 14 Nov. 1999. <http://www.mla.org/>.

Eliot, T. S. Introduction. *Seneca His Tenne Tragedies Translated into English*. 2 vols. Tudor Translations 2nd ser. 11–12. London: Constable; New York: Knopf, 1927. 1: v–liv.

Fox, Willard, III. *Robert Creeley, Edward Dorn, and Robert Duncan: A Reference Guide*. A Reference Guide to Literature. Boston: Hall, 1989.

Gerber, Helmut E., and W. Eugene Davis, comps. *Thomas Hardy: An Annotated Bibliography of Writings about Him*. 2 vols. De Kalb: Northern Illinois UP, 1973–83.

Giantvalley, Scott. *Walt Whitman, 1838–1939: A Reference Guide*. A Reference Guide to Literature. Boston: Hall, 1981.

Gibaldi, Joseph. *MLA Handbook for Writers of Research Papers*. 5th ed. New York: MLA, 1999.

———. *MLA Style Manual and Guide to Scholarly Publishing*. 2nd ed. New York: MLA, 1998.

Harner, James L. *English Renaissance Prose Fiction, 1500–1660: An Annotated Bibliography of Criticism*. A Reference Publication in Literature. Boston: Hall, 1978.

———. *Literary Research Guide: A Guide to Reference Sources for the Study of Literatures in English and Related Topics*. 3rd ed. New York: MLA, 1998.

———. *MLA Directory of Scholarly Presses in Language and Literature*. 2nd ed. New York: MLA, 1996.

———, ed. "Shakespeare: Annotated World Bibliography." Annually in *Shakespeare Quarterly*.

———, ed. *The World Shakespeare Bibliography on CD-ROM 1900–Present*. CD-ROM. Cambridge: Cambridge UP, 1996– .

Internet Movie Database. 29 Nov. 1999. <http://us.imdb.com/>.

Kinney, Arthur F. "The Art and Artifice of Renaissance Bibliography: A Review-Essay." *Analytical and Enumerative Bibliography* 6 (1982): 173–80.

Knight, G. Norman. *Indexing, the Art of: A Guide to the Indexing of Books and Periodicals*. London: Allen, 1979.

Krummel, D. W. *Bibliographies: Their Aims and Methods*. London: Mansell, 1984.

Literary Resources on the Net. Ed. Jack Lynch. 29 Nov. 1999. <http://andromeda.rutgers.edu/~jlynch/Lit/>.

Marcuse, Michael J. *A Reference Guide for English Studies*. Berkeley: U of California P, 1990.

Meserole, Harrison T. "A Bibliographer's *Apologia pro vita sua*." *A Selected Catalog of Books in the Seventeenth-Century Research Collection of the University of Wisconsin-Milwaukee*. Ed. Michael Allen Mikolajczak. Milwaukee: Golda Meir Lib., U of Wisconsin-Milwaukee, 1982. 61–70.

Meserole, Harrison T., and John B. Smith. "'Yet there is method in it': The Cumulative Shakespeare Bibliography: A Product of Project Planning in the Humanities." *Editing, Publishing, and Computer Technology*. Ed. Sharon Butler and William P. Stoneman. New York: AMS, 1988. 65–80.

MLA Directory of Periodicals: A Guide to Journals and Series in Languages and Literatures. New York: MLA, 1979– . (Biennial.)

Oakman, Robert L. *Computer Methods for Literary Research*. Rev. ed. Athens: U of Georgia P, 1984.

Patterson, Margaret C. *Author Newsletters and Journals: An International Annotated Bibliography of Serial Publications Concerned with the Life and Works of Individual Authors*. American Literature, English Literature, and World Literatures in English Information Guide Series 19. Detroit: Gale, 1979. Updated in *Serials Review* 8.4 (1982): 61–72; 10.1 (1984): 51–59; 11.3 (1985): 31–44.

Petry, Alice Hall. Rev. of *Robert Lowell: A Reference Guide*, by Steven Gould Axelrod and Helen Deese; *Bret Harte: A Reference Guide*, by Linda Diz Barnett; *Lillian Hellman—Plays, Films, Memoirs: A Reference Guide*, by Mark W. Estrin; *Sinclair Lewis: A Reference Guide*, by Robert E. Fleming with Esther Fleming; *William Sydney Porter (O. Henry): A Reference Guide*, by Richard C. Harris; *Louisa May Alcott: A Reference Guide*, by Alma J. Payne; *Louis Simpson: A Reference Guide*, by William H. Roberson. *Analytical and Enumerative Bibliography* 7 (1983): 58–72.

Reynolds, Michael M. *A Guide to Theses and Dissertations: An International Bibliography of Bibliographies*. Rev. and enl. ed. Phoenix: Oryx, 1985.

Roberts, John R. *George Herbert: An Annotated Bibliography of Modern Criticism, 1905–1974*. U of Missouri Studies 68. Columbia: U of Missouri P, 1978.

———. *John Donne: An Annotated Bibliography of Modern Criticism, 1912–1967*. U of Missouri Studies 60. Columbia: U of Missouri P, 1973.

Rollin, Roger B. Rev. of *Robert Herrick: A Reference Guide*, by Elizabeth H. Hageman. *Seventeenth-Century News* 42 (1984): 35–36.

Voice of the Shuttle. Ed. Alan Liu. 29 Nov. 1999. <http://vos.ucsb/edu/>.

Walker, Janice R., and Todd Taylor. *The Columbia Guide to Online Style*. New York: Columbia UP, 1998.

Washington, Mary A. *Sir Philip Sidney: An Annotated Bibliography of Modern Criticism, 1941–1970*. U of Missouri Studies 56. Columbia: U of Missouri P, 1972.

Appendix: Annotation Verbs

Compiled by Ken Bugajski

Accepts
Adapts
Addresses
Adds
Adduces
Advises
Advocates
Agrees
Aims
Allies
Allows
Analyzes
Annotates
Announces
Applies
Argues
Ascertains
Ascribes
Asks
Asserts
Assesses
Associates
Attempts
Attributes
Bases
Belies
Believes
Brings together
Calls
Catalogs
Categorizes

Cautions
Centers
Challenges
Characterizes
Charts
Chooses
Chronicles
Cites
Claims
Clarifies
Classifies
Collects
Commemorates
Commends
Comments
Compares
Compiles
Complains
Concentrates on
Concerns
Concludes
Concurs
Confirms
Confronts
Conjectures
Considers
Construes
Contains
Contends
Contests
Continues

Contrasts
Contributes
Corrects
Covers
Criticizes
Critiques
Deals
Debates
Declares
Deduces
Deems
Defends
Defines
Delineates
Demonstrates
Deplores
Derives
Describes
Details
Determines
Develops
Differentiates
Disagrees
Disassociates
Discerns
Discounts
Discusses
Disputes
Distinguishes
Divides
Documents
Doubts
Draws
Elaborates

Elucidates
Emends
Emphasizes
Encourages
Enumerates
Envisions
Equates
Establishes
Estimates
Evaluates
Examines
Excerpts
Explains
Explicates
Explores
Expresses
Favors
Finds
Focuses
Follows
Gives
Glosses
Groups
Guides
Highlights
Hints
Hypothesizes
Identifies
Illuminates
Illustrates
Includes
Indexes
Indicates
Inquires

Interprets
Interviews
Introduces
Investigates
Laments
Lauds
Links
Lists
Maintains
Mentions
Notes
Observes
Offers
Opposes
Outlines
Parallels
Perceives
Places
Pleads
Points out
Portrays
Posits
Postulates
Praises
Presents
Presumes
Prints
Probes
Profiles
Proposes
Protests
Provides
Puts forward
Questions

Quotes
Raises
Reassesses
Rebuts
Recalls
Recommends
Reconstructs
Records
Recounts
Redefines
Reexamines
References
Refers
Reflects
Refutes
Regards
Rejects
Relates
Relegates
Repeats
Replies
Reports
Reprints
Reproduces
Responds
Reveals
Reviews
Scrutinizes
Seeks
Sees
Shows
Sketches
Sorts
Specifies

Speculates
States
Stresses
Studies
Suggests
Summarizes
Supplements
Supports
Surmises
Surveys
Synthesizes
Takes
Tests
Theorizes
Thinks
Traces
Tracks
Translates
Treats
Tries
Underscores
Understands
Updates
Uses
Utilizes
Views
Writes